Chapter...
All Aboard

LIFE AFTER DEATH

From Vision to Voice- Manifested to Serve

Erica Barnes Grant

Table of Contents

Prelude... 3
Chapter 1
   Picking Up The Pieces... 9
Chapter 2
   Laying The Foundation.. 16
Chapter 3
   Dropping The Bomb.. 20
Chapter 4
   January 2017... 23
Chapter 5
   Let The Race Begin... 26
Chapter 6
   $FUNDS$.. 33
Chapter 7
   Runoff Time... 38
Chapter 8
   Unkown Workload... 45
Chapter 9
   Work Through It... 55
Chapter 10
   Rebuild And Focus... 60
Chapter 11
   Dr. Daria... 63
Chapter 12
   The Board Love.. 66
Special Thanks... 69

PRELUDE

    Well, one of the things I decided to write about in the twist of Life After Death was the school board. My cousin, Ethime, told me I would be on the school board, but I never imagined it would actually happen. He spoke so much life into me, even as he knew he was on his deathbed. It was so unfortunate—he had such a bright future he envisioned for himself, others, and especially his students.

    Back in 2009, I thought about the school board, as Ethime had mentioned I'd be on it because of my big mouth, always going up to the school and my concern for others needing to be heard. I didn't think much of it then and I definitely wasn't ready. Hey, I was on baby boy #4, running like none other with baseball, a new bundle of joy, and being a busy salon owner. DJ, my husband, was part owner of a club and life was cool!

    At that time, I had been a parent at the school for about five years. And since Ethime worked in the school system, he knew things that weren't always known to the

PRELUDE

public. As my oldest son, MJ's 5th-grade year came to a close, it was time to plan a big graduation party. He was headed to middle school and oh boy, we were excited. Until... at his graduation party, I met a guy.

This particular guy was the hotel manager where we were having the graduation party. As he came over and started telling me we needed to keep the noise down, he suddenly looked over and stopped talking. I was like, "Sir... are you OK?

He replied by asking me about my little cousin, Christian, who was walking up to me.

He said, "Is he with you?" and I waited before I answered.

I was like, "Ummmmm, WHY??" I didn't know if Christian had done something or what. But the guy was serious and asked again. I said, "Yes, he is. Why?"

He said, "Are you Erica? Ethime's little cousin?"

I said, "Yes... and you are?"

He explained that he was the band booster president and that Ethime was also his friend. I said, "OK. Great!"

Then he said, "But listen, I actually thought about reaching out to you..."

I'm still thinking, What is wrong with this guy? Energy switch. I asked him again, "Why? Reach out to me for what?"

He said he'd had a conversation with Ethime about his health and that he was not OK. I told him that couldn't

PRELUDE

be true. Ethime was fine. Just a few issues.

But the guy said, "No, listen. He said someone will have to die for him to live. He had to get a new heart."

Between mad and sad, I had to get it together. Mannnn! I immediately told the guy thank you and called Ethime. I explained what happened and told him I'd see him shortly. I called my family to be ready to head to Birmingham in an hour and a half. I called all the parents to come get their children. The sleepover ended early.

When we all arrived at UAB Hospital, we entered Ethime's room and everyone was so bubbly. I'm like, "Y'all, Ethime is sick." Again, they looked at me like I was being extra. I just went over and began talking with Ethime. He was sitting in a chair with his laptop out on the little food tray. He said he was planning band camp for the summer and getting ready to celebrate his fraternity's 100th conference.

I said, "AYE PLAYA! Stop playing with me!"

He said, "OK." He leaned toward me and whispered, "Cuz, I'm trying to wrap my mind around what these doctors are saying and stay positive."

I was like, "What?? What are they saying?"

He said, "Someone has to die for me to live..."

So now, in my mind, I had to be with him—listen and be a great cousin, lil sis, friend...

After we left, I cried, prayed, and vowed to do just that. The next day, I got up and called Ethime. He asked me to

PRELUDE

be true. Ethi come up and talk. An hour later, I was there. We talked a lot. One topic was MJ going to middle school and how there was a program called "No Child Left Behind." MJ was supposed to go to Eastwood Middle School, but Ethime said I needed to apply for No Child Left Behind. It was an option for a child to go to another school if the one they were attending—or planning to attend—was considered failing. At that time, MJ's next school was failing, so we sent him to another middle school.

Ethime asked for MJ to come see him, and he asked me again to stay involved in Tuscaloosa City Schools (TCS) and go back to school.

"Education is important. Being vocal in a professional, caring, and stern manner is needed in the school system. You will be on the board one day."

I went from serious to here he goes again...

I had just finished my cosmetology instructor program and he had finished his EDS from University of West Alabama. He desired to be a superintendent one day. So as he poured into me, I heard him loud and clear: he would be superintendent, and I would be on the board.

I heard him and he gave me so much insight over just a few weeks. On life, school, family, Greek life, but mainly, being a servant leader. I was intrigued. However, I wasn't really interested, especially not at that moment. So much on my mind. So much to deal with. I couldn't think about

PRELUDE

myself. And I didn't fully understand until Ethime's health hit a standstill.

During that standstill, he steadily poured into me. Then a decline came, and the days became long, unknown, and sad.

I went home one day to gather some things and do Chrishan's hair, Ethime's wife. While doing her hair, Ethime called and said the doctors told him he needed another surgery. Chrishan immediately left. He then called me and told me to come up there and pray with him, be there for his wife and boys.

"Do what I tell you," he said.

I asked why, and he replied, "Come on up, cuz. Remember all I told you? You're going to be straight." He loved to say that. He told me he loved me and to be careful. "Come on."

I left my beauty salon immediately and went by my mom's to pick her up. She was gathering a few things and I got on the road. We arrived maybe 42 minutes later and ran to the room to find an empty bed.

We flew to the nurses. They said he had to go on back to surgery. Days passed. He had not woken up from surgery, and his health was declining.

We all prayed. I talked to myself a lot. I talked to God. I talked to DJ, my dad, my family... Nothing eased me. The feeling of pain was on me, in me. There would be no more Ethime the way we knew him. I was still in disbelief

PRELUDE

that his life might end.

Well, we received a call for the family to come. His blood pressure had begun to drop. We camped around his bed, prayed, and all I could do was replay so many conversations in my head. With hope for a miracle, I knew God made no mistakes.

As bad as that pain got, I put myself in a chair and just became numb to it all.

Ethime transitioned to glory. And Life After Death began another story.

Psalms 34:18 (NIV): The LORD is close to the brokenhearted and saves those who are crushed in spirit.

Psalms 119:28 (NIV): My soul is weary with sorrow; strengthen me according to your word.

Matthew 11:28–30 (NIV): Come to me, all you who are weary and burdened, and I will give you rest. Take my yoke upon you and learn from me, for I am gentle and humble in heart, and you will find rest for your souls. For my yoke is easy and my burden is light.

Revelation 21:4 (NIV): He will wipe every tear from their eyes. There will be no more death or mourning or crying or pain, for the old order of things has passed away.

CHAPTER 1
Picking Up The Pieces

Chapter 1

To find my way and pick up the pieces was unimaginable.

Ethime was my cousin, homie, and mentor. A void in my life that I asked God how to bandage until I learned how to start healing. I was reminded of all the things I'd learned over the years from Ethime, but mainly those last days.

The last days, the last days... made ways. Ways of sacrifice, thinking of the great advice that led me to a servant life. With so much knowledge poured into me, the school board was on the to-do list... to at least fully check out. But first, I decided to enroll in school.

In 2013, I went back to college, our very own HBCU in Tuscaloosa: THE Stillman College.

So... not going to do that school board thing this term. I'll continue to pray about it and do my research. After much consideration, and things I saw in the school system I wasn't crazy about, I began to get more and more involved.

CHAPTER 1

In 2016, the school system voted to rezone—and it was a complete mess. Children were being shuffled across Tuscaloosa with no real logic. At first, I didn't think it would impact my family. But in time, it did.

Due to different issues, my son MJ had left his school under the No Child Left Behind Act and returned to his home school. We thought the transition was final, only to find out he had to return to the previous school again. He had finally settled in. He was thriving—playing sports, joining the band, making real progress. And now, they were pulling him back.

That's when the storm hit. "Lord, get us through this," I prayed.

I started attending school board meetings, desperate to understand how this decision was made and why it was affecting so many students—especially mine. How could they rezone us across the city like this? Who thought this was a good idea? When was the next meeting?

The more I thought about MJ's past experiences at that other school, the more unsettled I became. I decided to email every board member, asking for clarity and support. Days passed—no response. I wasn't trying to be a nuisance. I was just a parent who wanted to be heard.

At that point, I was willing to be whatever I needed to be for my child. Advocate, agitator, whatever it took. The following week, I prepared to attend the evening board

CHAPTER 1

meeting. I signed up to speak and anxiously waited for my turn.

Six o'clock couldn't come fast enough. When they finally called my name, I walked to the podium and smiled.

"Good evening," I said politely.

Then I shared my concerns—how MJ was being bounced around between schools at the last minute, and how I had just paid over $600 for his baseball spirit pack, only to find out he might not even be eligible to play.

Before I could finish, the board chair interrupted me. "Well," he said with a chuckle, "you can have this goody basket we got from the other school. It'll get you started with new school's gear."

He laughed.

I didn't.

It took everything in me not to walk up and throw that basket back at him. It was pure inconsideration—disrespectful on every level. That moment sealed it. It was time. Next election, I'd be lacing up my shoes for the run.

By January 2016, I was still going back and forth with myself. "Erica, don't start this again. You gon' back out like last time?" My stomach was in knots. The doubt crept in. I felt like people wouldn't understand me. I was just a parent. Who was going to take me seriously? But that voice of fear was soon drowned out by something stronger. I decided to prepare.

CHAPTER 1

One day, I walked into Family Dollar and picked up a spiral notebook for $1.59. I hesitated. Should I just get the 99-cent composition book instead? I also grabbed a calendar. Something told me this school board journey was about to take over my life.

I started a to-do list. At the top?

✓ **Pray. Seek God in every decision.**

Philippians 4:6–7 (NIV): Do not be anxious about anything, but in every situation, by prayer and petition, with thanksgiving, present your requests to God. And the peace of God, which transcends all understanding, will guard your hearts and your minds in Christ Jesus.

Did I mention I was a 34-year-old third-year junior at THE Stillman College, working toward a degree in business?

On that same list, I wrote:

- ✓ Stay in school and finish the marathon.
- ✓ Keep family a priority—so many moving parts.
- ✓ Maintain my business and continue serving my clients with excellence.

CHAPTER 1

I needed to be organized. After scribbling everything down on one page, I started searching online. I Google: *Alabama School Board Election*.

I clicked through a dozen links until I landed on the Secretary of State's page. There it was:

March 7, 2017 – Tuscaloosa City Municipal Election.

Fourteen months away—and I was already overwhelmed. My heart raced. I broke into a sweat. So what now? I picked up the phone and called the city.

Ringgggg.

"311, how may I help you?"

"Hi, I need information about the municipal elections." They transferred me to the city clerk's office, where I was connected to Mrs. Croom—a blessing in disguise. She walked me through everything I needed to know to qualify as a candidate.

From there I began my real preparation. I let all my clients know:

"Effective March 1, 2016, I'll be off on Tuesdays unless it is an emergency."

That wasn't an easy choice. I risked losing income. But if I was going to do this, I had to make room. I bought two folders—one for random notes, the other strictly for campaign planning. If you stay ready, you don't have to get ready.

CHAPTER 1

I remembered one of my favorite teachings from the Bible:

> **Matthew 25:1–13 (ESV):** "Then the kingdom of heaven will be like ten virgins who took their lamps and went to meet the bridegroom. Five of them were foolish, and five were wise. For when the foolish took their lamps, they took no oil with them, but the wise took flasks of oil with their lamps...."

The story continues—only those who were ready entered the feast. The others were left outside.

I wasn't going to be caught unprepared. Not this time.

CHAPTER 2
Laying The Foundation

Chapter 2

When I first thought about running for school board, I had no idea where to begin. I just knew I had a heart for students, parents, and educators. That's what I believed the position was truly about—and honestly, that's all I thought it was supposed to be about.

So I grabbed a pen and paper and started with what I knew:

#1 My purpose — to advocate for parents, educators, and mainly students.

That's it. That's what grounded me. That's what made sense.

> **Habakkuk 2:2-3 (KJV)**: And the LORD answered me: *"Write the vision; make it plain on tablets, so he may run who reads it. For still the vision awaits its appointed time; it hastens to the end – it will not lie. If it seems slow, wait for it; it will surely come; it will not delay."*

CHAPTER 2

Then came the pieces that made it real:

#2 My campaign slogan: "All Students Granted."
#3 My campaign manager: Shonte Baltes.
#4 Team? In the works.
#5 T-shirt and sign design? No clue yet.
#6 Who would make the signs? What would it cost?
#7 Pull a map of District 5. Call Kip Tyner, the city councilman.
#8 Find out where to put signs. Set up a campaign kickoff.
#9 Who's doing the phone calls?

The list went on and on. And then, like a brick wall, #14 hit me hard:

MONEY.

How? Who?? What??? I froze. WHAT MONEY FOR THIS CAMPAIGN???

I couldn't take from my family to run a campaign. That wasn't even an option. The thought alone made my heart race. So I did what I always do—I prayed. I took a quiet moment. Sat in stillness for about 20 minutes. Tears. Frustration. Surrender.

Then I went back to my pen and paper.

#14 – Ways to Raise Money

CHAPTER 2

I was blank on #14, however, I was believing God would fill it in. I kept going. I needed to learn how to file financial reports—maybe Mrs. Croom could help. I needed to map out the neighborhoods, identify liaisons, connect with churches, clubs, and write down what parents were concerned about. I needed to think about voter registration. Advertising. Radio. TV. Newspaper.

This was so much more than I ever expected. The foundation was being laid and though I didn't know how it would all come together, I knew I had to keep building.

CHAPTER 3
Dropping The Bomb

Chapter 3

So that was only the beginning. I started slowly, talking with just a few people. One of the first was Mr. John Gordon. He gave me a lot of insight into Tuscaloosa politics. I immediately told him, "I'm an advocate, not a politician."

He looked me straight in the eye and said, "Erica Grant, you are definitely a politician—and you're going to be one of the best advocates ever."
I didn't argue. I just listened. From that moment on, he became my go-to person for all things school board and campaign strategy.

"The right to vote is not only a privilege—it's our duty."
—John E. Gordon Sr., former member of the Tuscaloosa Board of Education (1992–2001)

Next, I called Kip Tyner, the city councilman for District 5. He was in his fifth term, and while some people tried to persuade me to run against him—WHAT?! I knew that

CHAPTER 3

wasn't my lane. I shared my true intentions with him: that I was planning to run for school board.

Kip was supportive. He told me I'd do a great job, but also advised me to talk to the incumbent when I was ready. I asked him to keep it to himself while I continued praying over the decision. The incumbent was Mr. Harry Lee. But I didn't reach out just yet. I waited.

As the months passed, that checklist I had made—the one that began with pure nerves—started becoming my reality. I started connecting the dots. I even had brief conversations with Dr. Daria, the superintendent of city schools, and Mayor Walt Maddox. Both of them encouraged me to go for it.

But Walt said something I'll never forget. It stuck with me. And no, I'm not sharing it just yet.

Before I knew it, it was January—time to qualify. Time had flown. There was chatter about the upcoming elections, but no one really knew I was serious. I had kept it quiet. But January 2017— That's when I dropped the bomb.

I finally contacted the incumbent, Mr. Harry Lee. I told him straight up: it wasn't personal. It wasn't about anything I thought he had done wrong. I explained my platform—how I wanted to build a stronger connection with the community and serve as a true advocate. He thanked me for the respect and the heads-up.

And just like that, I was in it.

CHAPTER 4
January 2017

Chapter 4

At the annual Martin Luther King, Jr. Breakfast, I announced my intent to run for the District 5 school board seat. The Mistress of Ceremony asked all who planned to run for office to stand and introduce themselves. I took a sip of orange juice, stood, and waited my turn. As I stood there, I could feel eyes on me.
When it was finally my turn, I whispered a quick prayer: "Lord, give me strength."

"Good morning! My name is Erica Grant, and I will be running for the school board for District 5."

The room was a little quiet at least it felt that way to me and then I heard clapping throughout the gym. Immediately after, people came up to tell me good luck. They said I'd do great and to let them know if I needed anything. And then came a lady with a question: "WHY?"

I looked at her and asked, "WHY not?"

She told me I should run for city council instead. She said another lady was running for the school board and that we could work together. I told her that my decision

CHAPTER 4

was made and to have a blessed day.

After the announcement, I started receiving all kinds of calls, inbox messages, texts—and then a call from a news reporter. I met with him later that day. He asked several questions, but when the article came out, nothing I said was published correctly. I learned early about the importance of checking and retracting articles. He listed me only as a "hair stylist," and the article itself was very vague.

He eventually revised the story and made it a little better.

> **1Samuel 16:7 (NIV):** But the LORD said to Samuel, "Do not consider his appearance or his height, for I have rejected him. The LORD does not look at the things people look at. People look at the outward appearance, but the LORD looks at the heart."

Even after all the announcing, interviewing, and remembering what Ethime spoke into me, I still felt unsure. A part of me wanted to wait until the next election cycle. But I knew I had to go ahead and qualify. The next day, I went down to city hall and it was official. Time to run a campaign. I pulled out my folder and got started with signs, shirts, and Facebook. The qualifying deadline closed, and there were four of us in the District 5 race.

CHAPTER 5
Let The Race Begin

Chapter 5

Philippians 4:13 (NIV): I can do all things through Him who strengthens me.

So, we had an incumbent, a lawyer, a retired teacher, and myself, "only a hairstylist." This race was about to heat all the way up. What I didn't understand was how four people could be in one race. I never came across that in my research on running for a political seat. I didn't understand how someone could win, or how the votes would be counted with that many candidates.

Still, I believed in a good, clean race. Keeping it classy. Keeping it cute.

In preparation, I started writing down the different neighborhoods I needed to visit. I began with a Saturday list—what to do, where to go, who would help. I ended up having the basketball team at that time come out and help. My daughter Paizley was just a little girl. We pulled her behind us in a wagon, and she held the cards we

CHAPTER 5

needed to hand out. My friends, my family, DJ, my mom, my dad, and different people from church all helped. We spread out in different neighborhoods every Saturday for the next six weeks.

During campaign season, there were also different community forums we had to attend. At these events, candidates would speak to residents and community leaders. The National Pan-Hellenic Council hosted a forum as well. At first, I was nervous, but I understood how important it was to our Greek community. That forum helped spark my interest in the service side of what they do. I'll leave that alone for now and maybe come back to it in the next book.

At every forum, all four candidates showed up. But at one particular event, the incumbent raised a point about "white flight." I wanted to know exactly what he meant. He explained that the school system had already gone from one high school to three. If we didn't take certain actions, many Caucasian families would leave the public schools entirely and form a separate system. That conversation made me want to learn more.

The incumbent told me that if I ever needed anything, just ask. He was "Free Will," he said. He had been on the board for years and was open to sharing what he knew.

Now, every time we had a forum, one of the young ladies I ran against would barely speak to me and looked at me a certain way. Of course, I can be cute and classy,

CHAPTER 5

so I didn't know what it was going to turn into. But our encounters remained calm.

On the campaign trail, I also did voter registration. A gas station in my neighborhood with high traffic allowed me to post flyers on their windows. I cleaned the windows regularly to keep them nice, and they kept my flyers up the entire time. I had signs all throughout Alberta City. People wore my T-shirts. At some of the registration events, people would pick up shirts and flyers too.

One night, my two best friends—Courtney and Tip—and I went out to a big event. Our campaign shirts were red, so we put on our red lipstick and took pictures. Then we went to every club that night. We put flyers on all the cars. It didn't matter what area people lived in. Somebody always knew somebody who lived in District 5.

That same night, I met a guy named Ant. I asked him where he lived, and he told me Alberta City. I told him,

"Okay, I need you to vote."

He said, "Girl, I can't vote."

I asked why.

He said, "I'm not registered to vote."

Right there in the club, over loud music while I was enjoying a drink, I asked him for his social security number. He gave it to me. I told him I'd do whatever I could to help him get his rights to vote. He was fine with it, and I got him registered.

CHAPTER 5

We picked up absentee ballots. We visited an assisted living facility. We even went to an apartment complex in our district that I hadn't known existed. A few people turned in other absentee ballots.

District 5 was huge, and I didn't realize how many people simply didn't vote. I learned that they didn't vote like they should. But I also learned that if enough people did vote, and no one received the majority, it could lead to a runoff. I kept hearing about runoffs but didn't fully understand what they meant at the time.

It was during one of those days, Mr. Kip Tyner helped me with some campaign logistics and told me about different neighborhoods in District 5 that I hadn't known about. We parked and walked through the neighborhoods. We talked with people. That meant a lot. He also told me to reach out to Reverend Clarence Sutton, who gave me advice based on his own experience on the school board. His son, Dr. Sutton, was a star principal. Both of them supported and encouraged me.

I was amazed. I had people who were really behind me. Just like I mentioned earlier, the news reporter who first interviewed me made the story vague and that rubbed me the wrong way. It bothered me, but I had to overcome that—just like I had to overcome so many other unexpected challenges on this journey. Eventually, he revised the story and reprinted what I actually said,

CHAPTER 5

which made it a bit better. I also became friends with another news reporter, Jabaree Prewitt, who always found my story interesting. From that point on, WVUA was one of the best stations to cover any political or school-related stories. I truly appreciate them for not stereotyping me or misrepresenting my story.

Day in and day out, we campaigned. We were so tired. We missed out on the fun things we normally enjoyed, but we stayed focused. My family, my friends, my church members, my children's basketball teammates and their parents—we all came together and campaigned hard.

What I hadn't mentioned yet was that this all took place in 2017, during my fourth year at THE Stillman College. Because of the campaign, I started failing one of my classes. I couldn't keep up. I just couldn't manage everything the way I wanted to.

With only a couple of weeks left in the race, we were still out campaigning. We were hitting every stop—even the churches.

I visited one church on a Wednesday night. Pastor David Gay opened his doors and had a packed house. He jokingly told me, "Don't just come around during campaign season." But he let me speak to his congregation.

I also visited Cornerstone Full Gospel Baptist Church, where Pastor Washington welcomed me. I asked Bishop Smith, who pastors a large church in District 5, if I could

CHAPTER 5

if I could speak to his congregation. He went above and beyond. He invited all the candidates to come and set up a station in his church so people could hear directly from us. He did fuss at me a little and told me to put my notes on an iPad.

And of course, last but not least, my pastor, Pastor Thompson. Every Sunday and every Wednesday, he announced to the church that I was running for school board. I appreciate him so much, and I'm also thankful for all the pastors, club owners, store owners, and everyday people who allowed me to advertise and gave me a chance.

CHAPTER 6
$FUNDS$

Chapter 6

Proverbs 13:11 (NKJV): Wealth gained by dishonesty will be diminished, but he who gathers by labor will increase.

In the last couple of weeks of the campaign, I had a big sign I wanted to put out, but I needed to figure out whose property I could place it on. I did my research, got the address, and found out the property belonged to a man named Mr. Pate. I found his information and left a message with his secretary. She later called me back and said he wanted to speak with me directly.

When we talked briefly, he said, "Hey, come talk to me and tell me what you got going on."

He mentioned maybe meeting at 4:00. I looked at my clock—it was 2:30. I thought, "What do you mean?!" But guess what... I was doing hair. I wrapped up what I was doing and went to see what he wanted.

He told me he appreciated me taking a stand, being a servant, and running for public office. He said he wanted

CHAPTER 6

to help me, and I said, "Okay, thanks." He offered his support and became a donor. He arranged a robocall and had mailers made for my campaign.

I don't think I've talked much about my budget, which really didn't exist. I had a little money, but I didn't know what all went into a campaign. So, his help came right on time. I mailed out as many flyers as I could to a certain area of District 5—not the whole district—but enough. I also sent out the robocall to voters from the last election. I just kept on campaigning.

Coming up to the finish line, I saw my opponents, their signs, their Facebook posts—all of it. I decided to make a video for the last couple of days of the race. The video featured Whitney Houston's "Greatest Love of All" playing in the background. I stood in front of The Alberta School of Performing Arts and spoke from the heart about why I wanted to serve on the school board. I shared how I wanted to be an advocate for educators, parents, and especially students. I wasn't concerned about being liked or getting in trouble. I just wanted things to be fair. And a little birdie once told me I was better in than out—that stuck with me.

Now we were getting close. March was here. Just seven days to go. Mr. Gordon was on the local radio station, the Jimmy Lawson show. All you heard was politics, politics, politics. That year, there were a lot of candidates in different districts. I stayed focused on mine.

CHAPTER 6

I didn't have a lot of money to buy ads, but I called in. Mr. Lawson was kind enough to let me speak briefly when they opened the lines. My mom fussed at me for calling in and not paying for an official ad, but I just did what I could.

Then came election eve. My stomach was in knots. They had to make sure the machines were working, the poll workers were ready, and all the paperwork was submitted—especially the financial forms. I could hardly sleep.

March 7th arrived. It was election day.

A woman named Greg, who used to do my hair when I was little, donated balloons. Someone else donated donuts. Someone else brought water. Mr. Johnson gave me more than enough shirts to pass out. We had shifts lined up at Alberta Baptist.

Rain was in the forecast, but that morning was beautiful. It was also my daughter Paizley's birthday, which made it an extra special day. She had her own shirt that said, "Vote for My Mommy." I got her ready for school, kissed her, and told her, "This year, Mommy won't be bringing cupcakes, but I love you." She told me, "It's OK, Mommy. You go and you win!"

I was so excited that morning, but I just couldn't get myself together. A friend put up a tent, set out chairs, and we were ready before the polls opened at 7:00.

It was time to let the race do what it was going to do.

CHAPTER 6

We learned how close we could campaign to the polling location, and people began driving around to check the numbers. All day, my stomach was torn up. I made a robocall, but I was also still calling people directly to get out and vote. Mr. Pate told me we could have a victory party that night. I said, "A victory party?"

We ended up having a big turnout. People were holding up signs. Miss Greg put balloons all down University Boulevard—red and white. It was beautiful. But around 5:30, the sky got dark. I panicked. "Oh my God! People are not going to come out in this rain and vote."

My dad was in the hospital that day. I told him not to worry about voting, but he insisted. He said, "I have to go. I got to vote for my daughter." The rain or the hospital wouldn't stop him from showing up.

By then, it was pouring rain. You couldn't even see in front of you. It slowed things down, but people still came out. It was crazy. I didn't move from that spot until 7:00 p.m. My family went back to the house to wait for the results. We passed out a little cake and just waited. The numbers started rolling in.

I still didn't fully understand how a four-person race worked. I had heard you needed 51 percent of the vote to win outright, and as the underdog, I didn't expect that. But guess what—I had 48 percent of the vote!

I was going into a runoff. And it would last another 6 weeks.

CHAPTER 7
Runoff Time

Chapter 7

So now we were in a runoff. Oh my God. I was sick about it, but happy at the same time.
Before diving into the next round of campaigning, I went to speak with my professor about what was happening. I scheduled a time to meet, and when I arrived, she wasn't ready. I waited patiently, taking notes on my next campaign moves.

When I finally went in, I explained what was going on and asked her to reopen the two assignments I had missed. I told her I could catch up and finish strong. She told me no. I tried to explain that failing the class would cause my GPA to drop. I would have to take an academic bankruptcy, which would cost me $7,000 because I'd have to withdraw from all my courses, even the ones I was doing well in. But she told me, plainly, that my runoff or my decision to run for office had nothing to do with her.

CHAPTER 7

As bad as that hurt, it made me stronger. It gave me even more fire—not just to win the runoff, but to graduate from college.

> **Exodus 14:14 (NKJV):** The LORD will fight for you, and you shall hold your peace.

I was now in a runoff with the retired teacher. A hairstylist versus a retired teacher. I was still the underdog, and I was doubted. One retired educator even wrote an editorial against me, saying I had no educational background and that the retired teacher was a better fit.

If losing $7,000 and being told by my professor that she didn't care about the election didn't light a fire in me, that editorial definitely did. I was on fire. I laced up my shoes and got to work.

The incumbent, Mr. Harry Lee, reached out to me and offered his support. I was thrilled. We became good friends during that time. He taught me so much about the school board and shared files and advice. He even came out to vote for me and encouraged others to do the same. I was so grateful for his endorsement.

Throughout the process, I learned about endorsements. I didn't receive any from voter groups. I had sat in multiple interviews and felt I did well, but I didn't get a single endorsement. I let it go. My greatest

CHAPTER 7

endorsements were from God, my husband, my children, my community, and Mr. Harry Lee.

So, here we go again—more forums, more Facebook posts, more door-knocking. But this time, it was personal. I wasn't proving anything to anyone else. I was proving to myself what God had already shown me, what Ethime had spoken over me.

For six weeks, I hit the ground running again—just harder. I knocked on doors, posted on Facebook, made phone calls, and revisited all the same places—but with more energy and focus. I hadn't thrown a victory party before, but this time I knew I wanted one. I knew it was going to be bigger.

One club offered to host a fundraiser for me. All the proceeds from the door went toward the campaign. Everywhere I went, people announced that I was running fo office. Those announcements helped. The visibility helped. I even returned to different churches to speak again.

A week before the runoff, I made a bold move. I decided to go to a neighborhood I had been advised not to visit—the Highlands. I had been told the people there wouldn't vote for me. I said, "Okay," but I didn't believe it.

That Sunday after church, in my Sunday clothes, I grabbed my flyers and told my husband, "Take me to the Highlands."

He asked, "You sure?"

CHAPTER 7

I said, "Yeah." And we went.
We stopped at a few doors. The first couple of people were nice. One man recognized me from working with my brother and put my sign in his yard. I kept going, focusing on corner houses—ones visible from multiple angles.

At one house, I knocked on the door, and a man came out. I later found out he was a local lawyer. He asked me my name and said, "Don't you see I already have a candidate?"

I said, "No, sorry. I didn't see it."
He said, "Well, look around."
I had to step back and walk to the side to see that there was another candidate's sign in his big yard.

I said, "OK."

Then he said, "I still want to hear your platform." I told him what I stood for. He was rude. I thought to myself, "We still have another week." I walked away and told my husband, "Forget him. Rude ass." And we kept it moving. Campaign day arrived again. I got up early, prayed, and voted. Then I went to the site and got set up. This time it was warmer, so we had coolers, water, and all the essentials.

At one point, an older lady needed water but refused to take it from me. Then she needed a chair, and even though I offered mine, she didn't want it. That didn't bother me spiritually, but it did make me pause and

CHAPTER 7

think, "Wow."

Then that same man—the one from the house with the sign—showed up campaigning for the other lady. I waved and spoke. He didn't. That moment could have pulled me out of character. But it didn't.

Now I understand what it means to be pulled out of your character. The old me would have gone off. But the new me is not fake—it's the version of me that listens, that stays calm, and doesn't let things shake me.
I ignored it and kept going.

We campaigned all day. I helped an older couple into the polling place. Someone called in a complaint, but I wasn't doing anything wrong. I was just helping.
Around six o'clock, we began preparing for the victory party—win or lose. I believed it would be a victory either way.

6:50... 6:51... 6:52... 6:53... 6:54... 6:55...

Then 7:10, 7:11...

The numbers came in fast.

There was a runoff in my district and another one. And when the results came in...

I WAS THE WINNER of the District 5 seat.
I couldn't believe it. My mouth dropped open.

Psalm 23:5 (NKJV): You prepare a table before me in the presence of my enemies; You anoint my head with oil; My cup runs over.

CHAPTER 7

Oh my God.

One of the men who had dismissed me during the campaign—the same one who once told me at a board meeting that I could "just have the goody bag"—walked right past me, looking to see if the other lady had won. He didn't even say hello. No "hey," "cat," "dog," nothing. Just walked by.

I didn't tell him the results. He had to go find out on his own.

We had our victory party that night. Mr. Pate helped host it, and an old friend of mine joined in. The event was at a hotel just five minutes from my house, right in the district. It was a grand celebration. Friends, family, people from the community all came. Mr. Tyner came, too. I hugged my husband and my children tight. They had sacrificed so much so I could run, and now we were here.

We made it.

It was a good time.

A grand time.

CHAPTER 8
Unknown Workload

Chapter 8

When you step into a new role like school board member, nobody really hands you a manual. What follows are a few snapshots—mini stories—from my first years in office. These are the moments that taught me, challenged me, and helped shape how I served. Every story mattered. And every story taught me something.

Swearing In & Meeting Mrs. House

And so that was April 6, 2017, but the real action didn't start until after we got ready for the inauguration. At an inauguration you have to get sworn in for your position. I knew nothing about that, but I learned very fast. After I won, I got a phone call from this lady and an email and all the things about the inauguration. I had so many instructions and things to follow. I didn't know that I was going to absolutely fall in love with this lady. She was like another mom. The sweetest lady ever! Mrs. Liz House. Oh

CHAPTER 8

we ended up talking and getting to know each other.

The Inauguration & Training Begins

So here we are at the inauguration. I have my babies with me, my mommy, my daddy, and I get sworn in. Wow! I never, you know, imagined all of this. Being on a stage with Judge England to swear me in, and after that, we had a little dinner with my family. Then it was time to hit the floor running. Um, I thought, well, we'll be off this summer. No. The next week, we had board training.

And in board training, you learn board etiquette. We learned a lot about different conferences we had to attend. We learned a lot about each other. We learned about different things with the school—things you'd never know unless you're actually on the board and talk to somebody who's been there.

But what I didn't know was how much we would have to learn about the budget, how much we would have to learn about construction, how much we would have to learn about personnel. It was a lot to learn and understand—like the organizational chart, how things go, who to call. They try to lay it out for us, but it's on us to receive it—being in group messages, reading different emails and understanding them.

Chapter 8

2017: 1st Big Project (MLK)

Job 23:13–14 (NKJV): But He is unique, and who can make Him change? And whatever His soul desires, that He does. For He performs what is appointed for me, And many such things are with Him.

One of the first big projects on the agenda was the remodel of a school that meant the world to me—a school I grew up in and carried so many memories from. That school was Martin Luther King, Jr. Elementary. I attended MLK from 1980 to 1993, and to this day, I absolutely love that school. I remember the classrooms, the hallways, the teachers—everything. So when I found out it was up for renovation, it hit home in a deep way. It wasn't just another project to me—it was personal.

As I got involved in the details, I quickly realized that a new voice needed to be heard in those conversations. There were so many layers to the process—blueprints, budgets, meetings—and I knew my perspective as both a former student and now a board member mattered. Being part of the decision-making team was a full-circle moment. One of my favorite contributions was helping decide to include quotes from Dr. Martin Luther King, Jr. throughout the building. It felt like we were honoring not just the name of the school but the legacy behind it.

Around that same time, we had the groundbreaking ceremony for Central Elementary. That was another exciting moment. We got to wear hardhats and

CHAPTER 8

participate in the ceremony—it felt big, like we were planting seeds for the future.

But it wasn't all fun and celebration. The construction side of things came with its own challenges. One of the most frustrating parts was the contract process. We'd vote on one amount, and then later, they'd come back asking for more. It was confusing and stressful, and I had to learn fast how to read between the lines and ask questions.

On top of that, we had many personnel matters come before the board like staffing issues, changes in leadership, decisions that affected real people. That part was heavy. I was learning that board service wasn't just policies and buildings—it was people's lives.

So Much More Than I Thought

In that first year, we hit the ground running. We started traveling to different conferences all over the place; some nearby, some far. You'd sit in rooms with people from all over the state, sometimes even across the country. They'd give speeches, hold workshops, share data, and talk policy. Some of it was eye-opening, things I had never thought about. Other times, I'd find myself zoning out because it just didn't connect. But I learned to take what I needed and leave the rest. That became my

CHAPTER 8

approach: absorb what will help me serve, and let the rest roll off.

I quickly realized, this board work wasn't just about showing up to vote. It was a full commitment. There was so much more involved than I ever expected:

- **Student Hearings** – by far the hardest part. Hearing about what these children go through and having to make decisions that impact their futures? That weighed heavy.
- **Board Meetings** – regular, detailed, and sometimes intense. You had to come prepared.
- **Conferences** – full days of sessions, learning how other districts handled similar challenges.
- **Community Events** – ribbon cuttings, prayer breakfasts, school visits—you had to be present and show support.
- **School Events and Celebrations** – these were the moments of joy: graduations, award ceremonies, and seeing the kids thrive.

It was a lot. More than I imagined. But each piece mattered, and I was determined to show up for it all.

CHAPTER 8

My Son's Graduation & the "Good Fight"

During 2017–2018, nothing major happened—except my baby, my first child, graduated in 2018. That was a big deal to me. Being on the board and watching him walk across that stage meant everything. He was the reason I started to fight the "good fight." What does fighting the good fight mean? To me, it means standing in the gap and going to war for the people who depend on us most: Students, Administrators, Parents and Faculty and Staff.

Why do I keep fighting? Because I believe in what's possible. I fight to make sure every child has a voice, every teacher is supported, and every decision reflects fairness and truth.

To stay in this fight, you have to:

- ✓ Do your research
- ✓ Ask the hard questions—even the ones you think you should already know.
- ✓ If you're unsure, don't just speak—seek clarity.
- ✓ Remember: there's too much at stake to get this wrong.

CHAPTER 8

Learning Through People & Loss

As a board, we started getting to know each other and working together. I began noticing changes in personnel—like principals leaving or other internal shifts. The more I served, the more I saw. One thing I appreciated was that Dr. Daria always kept us informed. We were never left in the dark, and I valued that.

I also started meeting people across Alabama—board members, superintendents, and others. I began doing more research. Anytime something came before us, I would read and dig deeper to understand.

Our CSFO became sick, and we had to make our first big hire. And guess what? The person we needed was already right under our nose. But instead, we launched this big national search and spent all this money. Looking back, I felt like it wasn't necessary. I know sometimes you have to go outside and do an external hire. But when someone is already doing excellent work, it feels like a slap in the face to overlook them. That was something I learned early—always try to give someone internal an opportunity, especially when they've worked their way up.

Speaking of working your way up, our superintendent is a prime example. He climbed the ladder himself, and now he promotes others who've earned it the same way.

CHAPTER 8

Learning Through People & Loss

As a board, we started getting to know each other and working together. I began noticing changes in personnel—like principals leaving or other internal shifts. The more I served, the more I saw. One thing I appreciated was that Dr. Daria always kept us informed. We were never left in the dark, and I valued that.

I also started meeting people across Alabama—board members, superintendents, and others. I began doing more research. Anytime something came before us, I would read and dig deeper to understand.

Our CSFO became sick, and we had to make our first big hire. And guess what? The person we needed was already right under our nose. But instead, we launched this big national search and spent all this money. Looking back, I felt like it wasn't necessary. I know sometimes you have to go outside and do an external hire. But when someone is already doing excellent work, it feels like a slap in the face to overlook them. That was something I learned early—always try to give someone internal an opportunity, especially when they've worked their way up.

Speaking of working your way up, our superintendent is a prime example. He climbed the ladder himself, and now he promotes others who've earned it the same way.

CHAPTER 8

Saying Goodbye

Our previous CSFO passed away. So did the incumbent board member, Mr. Harry Lee. He asked to see me before he passed. That moment was heart-wrenching.

So all of this happened in 2017, 2018, 2019. We saw so much, went through so much, and learned even more.

CHAPTER 9
Work Through It

Chapter 9

Romans 12:12 (NIV): Be joyful in hope, patient in affliction, faithful in prayer.

So here we are, in 2020—and oh my God, the pandemic! The COVID year is something none of us ever expected. (There'll be another book to tell you all about what happened to me.) Every month felt like 20. But when it came to the school system, I had to be strong. Push through, like none other.

We got the message that COVID was out, and we'd need to send students home early one day. Then the next day, they were going to be out for a couple more days. Then graduation got canceled. After summer, we had to come back wearing masks—mandated masks. It wasn't just us. This came down from the state, and the CDC gave insight on what schools should do. Every district made its own decisions. For us, we kept the masks—because we were living in the unknown.

CHAPTER 9

Nobody on earth really knew what was going on with COVID. We had speculations and specialists, sure—but we were board members, not doctors. What we did know was: we had to keep our children safe. I hated the mess, but it was what we had to do.

That year was hard. Personally and professionally. My dad passed away. I was attacked by a dog. My son got sick. I got sick—and ended up in the hospital for two weeks. I had to retake a class in my master's program. I graduated right after getting out of the hospital (we called it COVID pneumonia). I still have long-term health issues from it.I bought a building for my salon. Then they shut the salons down. Hard is actually an understatement.

On top of all that, I still had board duties—and those were top priority. It wasn't just about me or my children; we were responsible for over 10,000 students. Virtual school, academic loss, and the emotional toll on students—it was overwhelming. I can't even remember all of it, but I know I never want to go through anything like it again.

And just as we started to breathe again in 2021, something happened. We attended a board appreciation luncheon. We wore masks inside. When it was time to eat, we took them off. After eating, we took a group photo without them. I posted the photo on Facebook.

Next thing I know? Bad tags. Harsh comments. The

CHAPTER 9

internet lit us up. People called us hypocrites. Said we had rules for kids we weren't following. One man called us clowns. That hurt. I work to uplift and provide for students and parents—so that hit me hard.

I went live on Facebook to defend myself. I went back and forth with him. But our board chair, Mr. Eric Wilson, called me out:

"Erica, could you take that down? You don't go back and forth. You let them have it."

I said, "But they called us clowns!"

He reminded me: "You don't know them. It's different if it's a friend—but this ain't that. Social media drama won't fix it."

That moment taught me so much. I eventually stopped. But the damage had been done. And it got scarier. That same man showed up at our board meeting, sat and stared me down. Later, he even came to my salon. I have the video. His tag was covered, but you could see his face. He parked, looked like he was about to get out, then drove off. I called the police and gave them the footage. I don't know what he intended, but it scared me.

This is something I'll tell every board member—be careful. People will dish out hate, but they can't take the response. And sometimes, they go too far. That man could've come after me. After my family.

My husband was furious. Rightfully so. But we had to

CHAPTER 9

stay calm. One wrong move, and things could've ended badly. That season taught me to be still and let God handle things. Not everything needs a reaction. That lesson brought peace.

CHAPTER 10
Rebuild And Focus

Chapter 10

We finally got through 2021. Students returned to school. Learning started getting back on track. It was good to see children engaged again after such a long, chaotic time.

COVID took a lot from us.

People died. Families suffered. Some couldn't even say goodbye to loved ones with long-term illnesses. Some of the lives lost were our own students. One of the hardest losses for me: my good friend Kim. She was a secretary at one of our schools—one of the kindest people you'd meet. Rest in peace, Kim.

As we moved into 2022, our focus shifted to recovery. That year, we proposed a tax referendum—asking the city to raise property taxes to support raises for our educators, increased school security, continued extracurricular programs, nurses in every building, and more social workers for student support.

We wanted to ensure our system stayed innovative and safe. That meant more than academics. It meant

CHAPTER 10

emotional, physical, and mental health for our students.

We ran over 72 community meetings to share the vision. I presented at the Alabama Association of School Boards (AASB) about innovation in education. We had the chance to sell an old school building—but instead, we turned it into a resource center for Tuscaloosa. We partnered with local agencies to offer services all in one place.

Our district began to shine. We were named one of the Top 25 school districts in Alabama, four of our schools earned the honor of being designated National Schools of Character, and our academic scores improved across the board. To top it off, our superintendent was named Superintendent of the Year — a recognition that reflects the strength and progress of our entire community.

It was a proud season, but despite all that, the tax referendum did not pass—which brings us to now: we have to make reductions, and people are watching us. They're saying, "It's on the board now," as big decisions are being dropped in our laps—things like state-mandated phone bans, changes in graduation requirements, and budget cuts with staff reductions.

And while many of these are not local decisions, parents don't always understand that—it still falls on us. So now we ask: What do we do next? How do we protect our children, our teachers, and our schools with fewer resources? The fight continues.

CHAPTER 11
Dr. Daria

Chapter 11

It's not every day that you come across a leader who truly makes a lasting impact—not just on a school system, but on the people within it. Dr. Mike Daria is that kind of leader.

For over 28 years, Dr. Daria has dedicated himself to the Tuscaloosa City Schools, beginning as an English teacher in 1996 and serving in nearly every leadership role—from assistant principal to principal, executive director of personnel, assistant superintendent, and now, superintendent. His commitment to this district runs deep, and his leadership reflects both experience and heart.

One of the most admirable things about Dr. Daria is that his leadership doesn't stop at the office door. He's just as likely to show up at a school event in jeans as he is to lead a board meeting in a suit. He's present, visible, and hands-on—always willing to support students, staff, and even the Board when things get tough. That kind of presence makes a difference.

CHAPTER II

The strength of the relationship between Dr. Daria and the Board is rooted in three key qualities. He listens with purpose and respect, communicates consistently—reaching out weekly to check in, answer questions, and keep us informed—and leads with innovation, openness, and strength, balancing new ideas with a steady and consistent approach.

Personally, I want to thank Dr. Daria for the way he leads, the way he learns from all of us, and the way he shows up—literally and figuratively—for the people he serves. His vision and dedication continue to shape a stronger, more connected future for Tuscaloosa City Schools.

Galatians 6:9 (NIV): Let us not become weary in doing good, for at the proper time we will reap a harvest if we do not give up.

CHAPTER 12
The Board Love

Chapter 12

Each board I've had the honor to serve with has been truly amazing. Together, we've stayed on track—through more good than bad—and accomplished a great deal for our schools and our students. We've traveled together, attended conferences, shared meals with our families, and built relationships that go far beyond meeting agendas.

A special thank-you goes to Ms. Elizabeth House, whose incredible organizational skills have shaped the efficiency and professionalism of our board, our superintendent, and our entire system. She keeps us grounded, keeps us on track, and spoils us every holiday with thoughtful treats that bring joy to our work.

What makes this board strong is not the absence of disagreement, but how we handle it. If we disagree, we work through it behind closed doors to seek understanding and unity before stepping into the public eye. Still, we recognize the importance of transparency, and sometimes public questions are necessary for the

CHAPTER 12

sake of the community—and that's both legal and appropriate. For those moments, we lean into respectful dialogue, knowing our shared goal is always to serve students and strengthen our schools.

Disagreement doesn't divide us. It refines us. It pushes us to ask better questions, to listen more deeply, and to emerge with decisions rooted in collective wisdom.

This board has been a model of service-driven leadership. I am proud of the courage, compassion, and clarity each member brings to the table. We've supported each other in hard seasons and celebrated big and small wins alike. The love and respect we have for one another is real, and that's what makes our work not just effective—but meaningful.

To every board member I've served with—thank you. You've made me better, and together, we've made a difference.

John 13:35 (NKJV): By this all will know that you are My disciples, if you have love for one another.

So, with that, I was entering my third term with no opposition—and boy, was I excited!

I'm starting my third term!!

Special Thanks

Special Thanks

First and foremost, I give honor to God, the author of my purpose and the One who gave me the strength and grace to carry this vision through.

To my dear cousin and friend, Mr. Ethime Emonina—may you rest in peace. Your prophetic words planted the seed for this journey. This book is as much yours as it is mine.

To my family—thank you for your love, patience, and constant support. To my mom, thank you for being my rock. To DJ and the Fab 5, thank you for always cheering me on.

To the 2017, 2021, and 2025 Tuscaloosa City School Board members—thank you for the opportunity to lead alongside you. It has been an honor to serve. Special thanks to Superintendent Dr. Mike Daria for your leadership and partnership.

To my friends, colleagues, and clients—thank you for your encouragement, trust, and inspiration. Each of you has played a part in shaping this journey.

Special thanks to:

Dr. Shante' Morton, Rachael James, Dr. Lucretia Prince, and Kara Bernal—your belief in me helped carry this book to completion. Gabe Wallace, my first publisher, for giving me the push I needed to begin. Morgan Hale, my second publisher, for your creative excellence and going above and beyond.

To every reader—thank you. May this book serve as a reminder that when God speaks, we listen—and when we move in obedience, we walk in purpose.

Special Thanks

The 2017 School Board Members:
District 1: Matthew Wilson
District 2: Kendra Williams
District 3: Guy May
District 4: Patrick Hamner
District 5: Erica Barnes Grant
District 6: Marvin Lucas
District 7: Erskin Simmons
Chair: Eric Wilson

The 2021 School Board Members:
District 1: Karen Thompson-Jackson
District 2: Kendra Williams
District 3: Leslie Powell
District 4: Patrick Hamner
District 5: Erica Barnes Grant
District 6: Marvin Lucas
District 7: Erskin Simmons
Chair: Eric Wilson

The 2025 School Board Members:
District 1: Karen Thompson-Jackson
District 2: Kendra Williams
District 3: Leslie Powell
District 4: Clint Mountain
District 5: Erica Grant
District 6: Marvin Lucas
District 7: Erskin Simmons
Chair: Eric Wilson

True leadership is measured not by titles held, but by lives served and futures shaped.

Special Thanks

The Superintendent:
Dr. Mike Daria
(with author and school board member Erica Barnes Grant)

A heartfelt thank you again to Dr. Mike Daria for his unwavering leadership and support. Your dedication to the students, staff, and vision of Tuscaloosa City Schools continues to leave a lasting legacy

"Let us not become weary in doing good, for at the proper time we will reap a harvest if we do not give up."
—Galatians 6:9 (NIV)

www.ingramcontent.com/pod-product-compliance
Lightning Source LLC
Chambersburg PA
CBHW042332150426
43194CB00001B/37